How To Stop Talking Over People

The Ultimate Guide On How To Stop Interrupting People

Stephanie Mike

Table of Contents

Chapter 1

Interrupting

Interrupting during discussion is widespread. It can happen for a variety of reasons, including concerns about having enough time to make a point or the need to express one's opinion. In some circumstances, the people chatting may disagree on what constitutes an interruption. Whatever the reason for the interruption, it has a detrimental impact on communication.

Interrupting is not always impolite, and it can be acceptable or even useful in certain situations. However, most of the time, interrupting has negative consequences. The speaker may have planned to say something intriguing or noteworthy. However, you have discussed it, and you cannot be certain that they will repeat the information. If you can't wait for someone to complete speaking, the other individuals in the conversation may assume you lack self-control. This could be especially problematic if your coworkers or supervisor share this perception of you.

Most individuals believe that interrupting someone while they are speaking is impolite. It may even lead the speaker to assume you don't respect them. If the speaker believes you interrupted them because you do not appreciate or value their opinions, they may become furious. They may even withdraw from the discourse. If this happens, you may not only miss out on hearing what they have to say, but your relationship may also suffer as a result.

Interrupting the speaker can detract both parties from the flow of the conversation and the message that the speaker is attempting to convey. This can result in the loss of information that would have been sent had the interruption not happened.

A good conversation resembles a game of tennis. You take turns. The tempo may increase or decrease, but you continue to take turns.

Your tennis partner does not serve seven balls in a row and expects you to retain them all in play. They do not return your serve and then serve another ball while the preceding one is still in play. It's one ball at a time, moving back and forth, exactly like a wonderful chat.

As someone who is passionate about researching, studying, and learning about effective communication, I have numerous beliefs as to why people do not give equal attention. Here are a few of them.

Reasons for interrupting in a conversation:

- *It's what they learned as children.*
- *This is a cultural thing.*
- *This is a narcissistic thing.*
- *It's an insecurity issue.*
- *It's an exciting thing.*
- *It's a power play.*
- *It is a lack of awareness.*

Now, as much as I despise it in others, I must admit that I, too, have been known to talk over people. What I take pride in, however, is recognizing when I'm doing it and observing the effect it has on the other person. Sometimes it's part of the fun and excitement, at times they don't notice or care, and occasionally it's simply unpleasant and irritating. So it is critical to pay attention to how others respond. If it is not acceptable, I apologize for cutting them off, invite them to finish, and then SHUT UP while they do.

But what if someone else is performing the cutting? How would you handle this? That is determined by how essential the individual is to you or your want to be heard. If they are not important, let them go and move on with your life; but, if both are significant, it is beneficial to bring this behavior to their attention and inform them of how you are being affected.

John, could we just pause for a moment? I discovered that I couldn't finish my last three statements. I'm pretty frustrated right now. Could I please take a moment to finish what I want to tell you?

The response to this scenario will, of course, differ depending on who you're speaking with. However, regardless of how you may need to adjust the phrase, the aim is to convey your sentiments in an honest and sincere manner to begin a genuine conversation.

Chapter 2

The Art of Active Listening

I have always admired those with fascinating personalities. The ones who brighten a room, are the center of attention and naturally draw others in. I was always fascinated by what made them so appealing and captivating.

So I began to thoroughly observe them, and what I observed was astonishing. It turns out that the most charismatic individuals are not the loudest or most chatty. It is precisely the opposite! They say less and listen more. They closely listen to what others are saying and interact with them actively. They express genuine attention to what the other person is saying and provide insightful questions. It appears that they are concerned about the other person's feelings and emotions.

And when they do speak, their comments have weight. They speak passionately, and their words are more important than the rumbling of a thousand people. They tell other people exactly what they want to hear. It's no surprise that most influential people listen more than they talk.

Then there's Elon Musk, who takes negative input from his customers and uses it to better his goods. Consider the incredible inventions he has made and the fortune he has earned.

I, too, began to use this trait in my talks and was astounded by the results. People began to open up to me and express their feelings and opinions more openly. I developed significant ties and connections with others, and whenever I saw them, they greeted me with pleasant smiles.

Active listening has had a significant impact on both my personal and professional life. It has improved my communication skills and increased my empathy. I can understand people better and interact with them on a deeper level.

Listening skills also contribute to trust and trustworthiness. Someone feels respected and valued when they are being listened to. They believe their thoughts are important, which increases their trust and willingness to open out to you. Listening to others is beneficial because:

❖ *Gives you fresh ideas and insights.*

❖ *Helps you obtain respect and trust.*

❖ *Makes folks pay attention to you.*

❖ *Makes your relationships stronger.*

❖ *Improves your comprehension and empathy.*

Listening more strengthens your remarks and increases the likelihood that people will listen. It also helps in challenging situations where you need to keep your ideas to yourself. However, becoming a good listener is not a simple feat. It demands effort and practice. Here are strategies to become a better listener:

Put away distractions
Turn off your phone, close your laptop, and focus completely on the speaker. This demonstrates that you value their time and are truly interested in what they have to say.

Ask questions
Ask open-ended questions to clarify your comprehension and demonstrate your interest in the issue under discussion.

Avoid interruptions
Allow the speaker to finish their thoughts before you speak. Interrupting can be annoying and disrespectful.

Pay attention to nonverbal cues

Assess the speaker's body language and tone of voice. This can help you better comprehend their feelings and objectives.

Empathize

Try to grasp the speaker's emotions and opinions. This promotes rapport and improves partnerships.

Practice active listening

Make a concerted effort to listen to others and use the suggestions above in your daily interactions.

By using these suggestions, you might build your bonds with others, develop better communication skills, and increase your empathy.

Improving your listening abilities can have a significant impact on both your personal and professional life. You can establish more meaningful relationships, gain people's respect and trust, and broaden your empathy and comprehension of other people by honing your listening abilities. It's not simple, but with practice and effort, anyone can become a charismatic and compelling presenter.

Chapter 3

Mindfulness in Conversations

Years ago, if you had asked me if I could sit quietly for five minutes and do nothing, I would have laughed. My mind was a firehose of thoughts, with an endless inner dialogue narrating my likes and dislikes, a constant review of my to-do list, my judgments of those around me, and a constant contemplation on why prior events played out the way they did. The only time I got a break was when I was completely concentrated on a task that needed critical thinking. Writing code was my sole shelter, and I'd emerge from a long coding session completely unaware of how much time had passed since I was so concentrated on the task at hand.

That was before I realized what meditation might do. The route to discovering meditation was neither magnificent nor enlightening. It was paved with deep anguish. The death of someone close to me in an automobile accident had put me in a state of grief I had never experienced. All of the other things that had previously occupied my head had been replaced by persistent waves of grief. Though I tried to entertain fresh ideas or concentrate on activities, they were swiftly overshadowed by waves of grief.

Grief, in all its darkness, provided an unexpected revelation. With the crushing weight of loss, my attention was no longer occupied with the normal parade of trivial concerns. There was just space for my loss's agony. As my healing progressed, I began to wonder if something less terrible could provide the same solace as mourning.

This question prompted me to meditate. It began as a means of healing, an optimistic attempt to regulate the grieving thoughts that were consuming my head. As an entrepreneur and business leader, my strategy has always been about control and attaining precise goals. Why couldn't I regulate my thoughts without diverting myself by concentrating on a certain task?

My meditation practice evolved over time into a useful tool, a buddy, and a haven of peace in the midst of chaos. I will not pretend that I attained Zen-like tranquility immediately away. Far from it. In the beginning, it was an awkward dance with my thoughts. But with each day, as I sat in solitude, simply breathing, I began to experience a sense of inner calm.

I observed a significant difference in my interactions with others after practicing mindfulness. My talks become richer. I was actually listening and not preparing comments while others were still speaking. I was entirely there, and in that presence, I discovered a level of connectedness that I had never experienced before. I improved my listening skills and actively participated in serious dialogue, which was unusual for me in the past. My chats were interesting and in-depth.

The power of being present gradually weakened. Mindfulness, as I've come to understand it, is more than just silencing the exterior world; it's also about quieting the inner chatter. By regulating my thoughts, I gained clarity, allowing me to make more focused decisions.

The journey to mindfulness goes beyond meditation. It pervades every moment, from the ordinary to the deep. It serves as a continual reminder that each minute is a gift that should be enjoyed rather than squandered.

My journey with mindfulness and meditation has been anything but straightforward. There have been detours, pit stops, and barriers on the way. But with each stride over the last six years, I've developed a better understanding of myself, a clearer perspective on the world, and a deeper respect for the moments that make up life.

Though I have a devoted meditation practice every morning for around 15-20 minutes after waking up, I notice that a contemplative state pervades my entire day. This, to me, is when mindfulness reveals its genuine potential. I pay considerably more attention in meetings, not because I am "zoning out," but because I am actually present and listening. I'm a lot more engaged with those who are close to me, genuinely interested and fascinated by what they say and how they present themselves.

Conversation and communication are fundamentally about the exchange of energy and ideas. Being open and receptive helps me to cherish and respect the folks with whom I've had the privilege of spending a small period of time.

For anyone thinking about taking this journey, keep in mind that you don't need a nice cushion or an exotic getaway. All you need is the resolve to be there for yourself every day. I can tell you that the benefits are worth every moment.

Chapter 4

Communication Skills

The best communicators listen intently to others and convey information in an understandable manner. They can receive verbal and nonverbal feedback while also sharing their thoughts and opinions in an inclusive manner.

Regardless of the communication method, effective communication requires a relationship with people. It's a dance in which you occasionally make surprise movements with your partner. This means that the most potent ability you can use is being in sync with your audience. It entails first understanding and communicating with its demands, and then responding to real-time input. It entails engaging in the conversation that your listeners want to have.

How to Improve Your Communication Abilities

The best messages are usually straightforward. If the message is not understood correctly, there is no point in communicating in any way—spoken, written, formal, or informal.

High-level communication skills include communicating effectively, retaining interest, and including all your team needs to know. Here are ways to communicate effectively:

Keep your audience in mind
Tailoring your messaging to your audience's interests will automatically increase their interest and engagement. Piquing their attention by speaking directly to what is important to them will automatically increase their willingness to understand and interact with the content.

Use a single word instead of ten

Even the most interested and passionate audience will eventually become bored. It will be simpler to understand and recall your message if it is clear and simple. Recall that although they are hearing it for the first time, you already know exactly what you are going to say. Keep things simple.

Consider the finest approach for delivering your message

If the information you're communicating isn't urgent, send an email or a memo. This is especially important for communicating expectations. Written communication allows your audience more time to analyze, reflect, and ask follow-up questions. They will also have an easy-to-access record to refer to.

Get them involved

If you've ever held a position as a manager, coach, trainer, or teacher, you know that one of the greatest ways to learn new information is by teaching. Ask them for their opinions or to assist in educating their colleagues about new ideas and procedures.

Use face-to-face contact whenever possible

Face-to-face communication provides numerous layers of information to each discussion, whether it's between two individuals or two hundred. Face-to-face interaction frequently produces a synergy that is hard to duplicate in another setting. Here are some ideas for maximizing in-person interactions with your team:

Make eye contact

If you're wondering if your message is getting through, a few indicators provide more feedback than eye contact. You can readily detect if the person you're conversing with understands you, is distracted, worried, or puzzled, all of which are lost in digital communication.

Request feedback

Not sure if they got it? Ask! A strong strategy is to have individuals repeat back their version of what you just stated. Often, this can boost recall, and immediate comprehension, and reduce future

misunderstanding. You can also ask them to get in touch with you
with ideas on how to sharpen your communication and presenting
abilities.

Read nonverbal clues
There are several forms of nonverbal clues. Yawns, fidgeting, and
gazing about the room are frequent indications that your audience is
not paying attention to what you're saying. If you observe this, do not
take it personally. Try asking them to share their thoughts, review
earlier points they may have missed, or adjourn until a later time.

Minimize distractions
If you're conversing with someone or a group in person, keep
distractions at bay by removing any superfluous technological
gadgets from the environment. Keep attendance to those who need
to be present, and avoid scheduling at times when people are likely
to be preoccupied with something else, such as shortly before the
conclusion of the day or right before lunch.

Chapter 5

Having Empathetic Conversation

I'm not sure about you, but I can occasionally get caught up in a heated debate without realizing it. Writing about and practicing empathy is a constant process, much like life. There are highs and lows. There are instances when you are better suited to the work than others. For me, bringing empathy into each conversation is an active principle. To put it another way, it is not instinctive. I need to ponder on the circumstances and discipline myself in order to concentrate more on the person in front of me.

Thus, it occurred to me that it could be useful to define what it means to have an empathic discourse. To begin, there are several types of discussions. For example, it could be a brief conversation with a cashier or the initial greeting with your partner in the morning.

Empathy can be especially useful in these less consequential meetings. But what about having a longer conversation with an individual, friend, or stranger, on a topic that is not trivial and where the other person has a different point of view? This needs a more determined effort, as it necessitates self-monitoring, thorough listening, and maintaining a meta viewpoint.

One of the most important concepts I've learned is to consider 'us' when engaging in a conversation with someone. In other words, how can one person conversing with another generate a third, presumably superior presence? The other aspect of contradiction is the necessity to strike a balance between your desire to listen and learn, as well as your ability to change your opinion, and having a conviction, or holding a coherent and congruent point of view that you feel compelled to maintain. It's about carrying your ideas softly. Yes, to adhering to your guns while also realizing that you can let them go. The crux of the notion is to understand which items are non-negotiable for you.

As we continue to investigate the concept of having an empathic discourse, it is critical to understand how we may evaluate empathy beyond subjective and perhaps ambiguous limits. It's important to understand the difference between sending and receiving empathy. On the one hand, there is the listener's empathy quotient, which is inherent in his or her intents.

This indicates that for everyone or any business that wants to be empathic, it's about one's effort and goal, to some extent, regardless of how much empathy the target expresses explicitly. In other words, a marketing team that creates and develops a shampoo bottle that does not slip through a soapy hand in the shower may necessitate a level of empathy that the person in the shower is unlikely to perceive, if not stated.

Nonetheless, empathy was being demonstrated. On the other hand, there is the receptor for empathy. To what extent does the 'target' of the empathy feel you were empathizing? This is the most commonly used scoring method, however there are no actual means to measure on an absolute scale.

The context in which the conversation takes place is quite important since it can influence the ambiance. It will undoubtedly have an impact on your degree of concentration, your capacity to hear well, the types of distractions that surround you, such as your cell phone, children playing, public space, and, finally, your sense of privacy. Before engaging in any meaningful conversation, one must be aware of the context. This contains two more crucial factors:

To what extent are you personally present? What is your current level of anxiety or stress? How comfy are you?

How much time do you both have for this conversation? Is there a hard close, and what happens next, i.e., how much will that incident contaminate your ability to be present throughout the conversation?

The first step is crucial because if you don't check in with yourself, you'll struggle to control your emotions, and ego, and listen. For the second point, having or giving time indicates that neither individual feels compelled to express all of his or her thoughts. When an interview or conversation is limited in time, it becomes more about pushing one's talking points, which impedes a free and real exchange of ideas.

After checking in with oneself, the next step is to assess your own attitude/mindset. What are your true intentions in this conversation? Do you actually want to know what the other person thinks? Are you curious about how that person got to have his or her beliefs? Are you willing to listen without judging? Can you listen without interrupting? And, most importantly, do you believe you have the ability to change your mind? The answers to these questions will vary depending on the issue and the person.

If we're looking into what makes an empathic conversation, that doesn't mean we should have a kumbaya-style meeting. If your goal is to persuade or win over the other person, it is a very distinct and appropriate beginning point in a conversation. However, it is important to recognize that it is possible to want to persuade someone while also having empathy. In fact, the more you comprehend the other person's point of view, context, and emotions, the more equipped you will be to persuade them. Any negotiator will understand this. Being sympathetic does not necessarily imply being pleasant. It does not imply being weak or giving in. Just as dissolving a heated conversation may be the greatest option, exercising empathy does not require you to agree with one another.

When two people have an empathic conversation, they both feel heard and are better able to understand each other's perspectives and emotions. I've witnessed the ability to bond despite our differences once we've all felt heard. When meditating on what you've heard, you may also observe the emotions displayed, if suitable.

To have an empathic and productive discourse about a difficult topic, two people should share several basic beliefs. Ideally, this is something that can be directly communicated. More likely, it is inherent in the exchange.

Locate a convenient and relatively tranquil location.

Make sure both parties have enough time to engage in a longer discourse.

Be self-aware. Check your mental state before the talk begins. Consider how and why you may have non-negotiable views, as well as where you may be able to dispute them.

An empathetic discussion is a two-way communication in which both people sincerely want to listen to and understand each other. If at all possible, state this up front in the trade.

Reformulation is necessary, at the very least, when there is uncertainty about understanding. However, it is beneficial to reformulate without judgment throughout the discourse, staying with and delving further into the other's train of thought. It's not necessary to put the other person on the defensive in order to listen with empathy.

Continue to think of the conversation as a partnership in which you are both committed to learning from one another.

Always use courteous language.

Keep an eye out for words whose definitions could be misinterpreted.

Keep track of any agreements you make out loud.

Agree to end the talk if it is getting nowhere or becomes too heated.

An empathetic discussion is a two-way exchange in which both parties sincerely want to understand the other.

Chapter 6

Managing Conversations in Different Settings

Work

In the digital age, digital workers are frequently more comfortable conversing behind a screen than face-to-face or vocally. You may use your smartphone to send messages or emails, as well as to chat with people, and you are likely to express your ideas using emojis in these tools, correct?

However, according to recent statistics, there is a big disparity between how good college students and recent graduates believe their oral communications are and how employers perceive such skills. While most young people believe they communicate effectively orally, less than one-third of employers agree.

The importance of good verbal communication
Communication effectiveness is based on a variety of elements. From what you say and how you say it to nonverbal communication, writing skills, and even your entire look, all of these factors influence how you share, receive, and transmit information.

In the digital age, oral communication abilities on the job are still critical. There will be several scenarios at work where you will need to apply these talents. From business meetings to product or service seminars; when you need to give a presentation or lecture to colleagues or clients; and even in everyday discussions.

When you communicate well verbally, you are better able to avoid time wastage, misconceptions, miscommunication, and conflict. And control how others perceive you. In the professional setting, where "time is money," acquiring strong oral communication skills means you are better equipped to transmit accurate and relevant information quickly and efficiently, which ultimately leads to better outcomes. You prevent the confusion that can result from email or text interactions where meaning is skewed. You also communicate your professionalism and proficiency to others, particularly your bosses.

So, how do you improve your oral communication abilities in order to perform better at work and advance your career? There are several work circumstances, but the following are four of the most typical. We provide tips on how to communicate more successfully in certain scenarios, which you may adjust to suit other types of conversations.

Whether you're holding a meeting with coworkers or attending as a participant, you'll want to convey your ideas simply, crisply, and immediately. If you speak too little, you risk failing to convey your message. If you ramble on for too long, others may lose interest and stop paying attention. Take a moment before speaking to consider precisely what you want to say. This can help you focus better and avoid chatting too much and confusing people. Generally speaking, it's a great communication habit to develop to consider before you say. Also, you may need to wait to add your opinion; establish a bullet list of the points you intend to make. This helps you stay on topic and not feel like you have to cut someone off.

You will most likely have to give a presentation at some time in your professional career. If you are not naturally comfortable speaking in front of others, you will have to deal with the nerves and stress that can accompany public speaking. It is critical to plan and practice ahead of time in order to feel more confident, which will lead to a sense of serenity. Again, be clear about what you want to say, and the important concepts or messages you need to express, and allow plenty of time to create the presentation concisely. Try to utilize brief phrases and sentences to concisely summarize each idea. Aim to speak as slowly as possible. Even if you are scared and want to finish the presentation as soon as possible, remember the value of each major concept and don't rush. You'll do the task faster with less confusion. And more professionally.

Workshops and ideation sessions are commonplace in the workplace. These are the areas where ideas can be tested, prototyped, developed, or discarded. If you're going to a workshop, think about why you're there, what you want to accomplish, and what the ultimate goals are. Again, this will allow you to focus on your objectives and clarify your communications. Recall to avoid interjecting and to show consideration for other participants. You can communicate effectively with others by paying attention to what other people are saying and thinking about what you need to say. Make sure the message you convey is succinct and direct. As you build your reputation in the workplace, how you learn, progress, and contribute to the company's growth will influence how others perceive you.

Conversations occur frequently in the workplace. Whether they are directly work-related or off-topic interactions among coworkers. So think of discussions as both a direct function of getting your job done and a means of developing positive and vital relationships with coworkers.

Good verbal communication is mostly based on good listening skills; you must grasp what someone is saying in order to answer appropriately. Don't be hesitant to repeat what someone says to ensure you understand and that you're both thinking the same thing. Use language that shows respect for the other person's point of view, even if you disagree. Assisting others verbally involves attentive listening.

When communicating in the office, it is critical to be respectful of your coworkers and remain professional even in the most informal of situations. Finally, try to be confident in your communication. Avoid making statements that sound like inquiries, but be careful not to come out as arrogant or confrontational. Be aggressive in your communication while listening and empathizing with others. Confidence in yourself and your words implies that you believe in what you're saying and want to follow through.

There may be several ways you are unwittingly isolating yourself from group conversations. When people are apprehensive or uneasy, they frequently engage in safety behaviors to reduce the danger of saying the wrong thing, being ridiculed, or being embarrassed. Safety practices might exacerbate anxiety while keeping you calm and restrained. In this way, arbitrary regulations can prevent you from participating in a group conversation and leave you feeling excluded.

Here are some instances of superfluous regulations that can make you feel like an outsider in group discussions:

- *Never interrupt anybody.*
- *Do not talk about yourself.*
- *Edit and rehearse what you say.*
- *Do not disagree with individuals.*
- *Keep your distance.*
- *Come late, go early.*
- *Be too cheery or positive.*
- *Until you are spoken to, keep quiet.*
- *Be seen but not heard.*
- *Leave your emotions out of it.*

How to speak in groups

Feeling excluded from group interactions can be caused by a lack of awareness about where, when, and how to include yourself. The following are some of the finest ways to participate in a group discussion. They may make you feel included, whether in a huge or small group. You can use these abilities to learn how to communicate with a group of friends, coworkers, or individuals you've recently met.

When you first go into a group conversation, make sure to meet everyone. If they are speaking in groups, you can greet them all at once by stating, "Hi everyone!" or, "Hey guys, what did I miss?" If they are having side conversations, you may approach folks individually and say hi, shake hands, and ask how they are. Greeting individuals in a courteous manner sets a great tone for the conversation and increases the likelihood that they will want to include you.

Speaking up becomes more difficult the longer you wait. Anticipation can lead to nervousness and even silence. You can break this pattern by speaking up immediately, within the first minute or so of joining a conversation. This helps to generate momentum, increasing the likelihood that you will continue to speak up during the conversation. If you're not sure how to be heard in a gathering, the best method is to project your voice and talk loudly and clearly.

While you may believe that speaking is the only way to participate in group discussions, listening is just as vital. Being an active listener is paying complete attention to the person speaking and showing interest by making eye contact, nodding, beaming, and repeating significant points of what they said. Paying more attention to other people than yourself may help you feel less uncomfortable and self-conscious.

Another approach to participate in a group discussion is to encourage or agree with the individual speaking by making eye contact, nodding, smiling, or using verbal encouragement like "yeah" or "uh-huh. People respond well to this type of encouragement or support, and they are more inclined to speak directly to you or give you an opportunity to speak.

It's better to build on the topic of the group conversation when you first join it than to start a new one. Being too quick to change topics can come out as aggressive or threatening to others in the group.

Instead, pay attention to what is being said and try to find a way to build on the current issue. For example, if they are discussing a basketball game, ask "Who won?" or say, "That was an incredible game."

You may not be able to say anything unless you interrupt. If you do not get a chance to speak, it is acceptable to interrupt, as long as you are courteous about it. Saying, "I just wanted to add a thing," or, "That made me think of something," is a simple and effective way to enter a conversation. Remember to speak out and project your tone so that everyone in the circle can hear you.

Nonverbal gestures are effective communication tools that are less intrusive than interrupting or talking over someone. Because the person speaking has the authority to delegate turns to others, consider raising a finger or hand while maintaining eye contact with the person speaking to indicate that you have something to say. If they receive the signal, they will usually give you a turn once they have finished talking. Turn signals can also be used to steer a group back to or transition between subjects.

People in groups are obliged to hold opposing views and ideas. These differences can often lead to tension or disagreements between people, therefore it's preferable to speak up when you agree with someone than when you disagree. People bond more over similarities than differences, so concentrating on the common ground will help you relate and connect with others. If you frequently feel excluded from group discussions, finding common ground can help you feel more included.

Groups thrive on energy, thus being excited can help you boost the energy of the group. Being enthusiastic is another effective approach to attracting others with positive energy. Try reading the energy of a group and increasing it by 10%. You can boost your vitality by speaking more passionately, enthusiastically, and expressively. Enthusiasm is contagious, therefore using passion and energy is an excellent method to leave a lasting impact and positively contribute to a group.

It's crucial to realize that a group is made up of multiple individuals, each with their own set of emotions, fears, and discomforts. When one member exhibits signs of discomfort (e.g., avoiding eye contact or shutting down), it is critical for other members to shift the conversation in another direction. Aim for themes that get the most people talking and involved, rather than those that shut people down, make things quiet, or cause people to turn away. Learning to read social cues will help you understand what to say and what not to say in gatherings.

Being honest with oneself is essential for self-esteem and the only way to have meaningful connections. While you may feel compelled to agree with everyone and become a social chameleon, this will prevent others from truly getting to know you. If your goal is to speak without talking about yourself, you may end up with an engagement that lacks authenticity. Being true to your feelings, opinions, and preferences can make it simpler to participate in group conversations without feeling the need to modify yourself simply to fit in.

Stories are an excellent method to communicate more about yourself without boring or disengaging your audience. A strong narrative needs to include an introduction, a pivotal moment, and an ending. If something in the chat brings to mind a hilarious, intriguing, or strange experience you've had, consider sharing it with the group. Good stories have a lasting impression on individuals, and they can even inspire others in the group to open up and share their own experiences.

At a social function, don't be afraid to strike up a side discussion with someone with whom you share a lot of interests. Consider addressing someone who appears to be feeling left out or excluded and is failing to fit in with the group. Approaching them and striking up a dialogue can make them feel more comfortable. Starting a one-on-one conversation can help an introvert feel more at ease.

Certain topics, such as religion and politics, have not been discussed openly enough to demonstrate that difficult disagreements may be resolved successfully. As a culture, we rarely see a dispute that does not turn ugly: differences of opinion, particularly on social media, frequently deteriorate into negative character assumptions and personal assaults. Many of us were told not to talk about bad emotions and other unpleasant things. We were instructed to avoid conflict and maintain the peace. We don't know how to conduct these hard conversations without eliciting negative emotions and character assassinations.

Sometimes these conversations are required to demonstrate that you care enough about someone to openly express your feelings and move the relationship ahead; other times, they are not. Or in the correct place or scenario. How can one discern when to speak and when to remain silent?

One of the first steps is to determine your point of view and why you hold it. Consider whether you are open to having this talk and willing to hear another person's point of view. This isn't a university lecture hall: a conversation isn't just about pouring your opinions all over someone and expecting them to remain mute.

Understand your own emotional boundaries and whether you are actually willing to hear the other side of the story, which may include a conversation about your conduct. Is the other person prepared for this conversation, or do they lack the emotional space to comprehend it? Can you convey your emotions in a calm and sensible manner without damaging their character? If not, there is a clear line you should not cross unless you are confident you can do so respectfully.

Being conscious of these boundaries and clear in your perspective will help you navigate the conversation while respecting the other person's sentiments.

Conducting Difficult Conversations

Determine when to talk and when to wait. Emotional urgency leads you to believe that specific talks have an expiration date: Silence may be protective and even beneficial in relationships; communicate later, when the problem has lost its emotional immediacy. Some interactions require a contemplative mindset. Is this festive setting the best place for this conversation? Can you wait until another time for this? No one will listen to you if you are ranting in the midst of an emotional tempest. Perhaps arrange a coffee discussion or a walk after the holidays to go through perspectives apart from the immediate emotional reaction.

If your debate is going nowhere, simply agree to disagree

Sometimes you'll be able to reach an agreement, but other times you may have to end the disagreement without a resolution. You don't have to sacrifice your position. However, you might have to allow the other person to keep expressing their viewpoint. It's possible that the conversation will never come to a complete resolution. In that case, you must be at ease with the prospect and make sure the other party is aware of your motivations.

Speaking your own truth and actively listening are equally vital.

Being heard and validated is very powerful. A productive discussion is hardly what you would find in a Rocket Science class with a hundred students and a dull professor reading off a PowerPoint. It is not appropriate for the other person to remain mute while you talk endlessly about your thoughts and opinions.

Nonverbal Signs of Active Listening

Show them you're listening by nodding your head and making eye contact, but not direct eye contact for too long, because this creates a creepy discomfort that triggers our fight-or-flight response.

When they say something, validate it with sounds or phrases like "Mmmhmm," "Okay," or ""That makes sense, that's logical, that's understandable, or I grasp your point."

When using these acknowledgment sounds, keep your tone and body language under check. Using a sarcastic tone of voice and a standoffish stance, such as crossed arms, tapping your foot, and/or tightening your jaw, will not convey to the person that you are listening to them or appreciate their thoughts.

<u>Avoid the blame game</u>
Nobody hates being suspected of purposely harming a loved one, and these charges only exacerbate negative feelings and activate the self-defense mechanism. By accepting responsibility for your sentiments, you can demonstrate to the other person that you own them. It doesn't matter what their goals were when you sensed them. You own them. Taking responsibility for your feelings, rather than making it appear as if the other person intended to hurt you, fosters understanding and develops the emotional bond.

<u>Pay attention to the evidence that supports your position</u>
Do not succumb to your emotional reactions to mounting strain. When these discussions evolve into heated disputes, it might be helpful to keep the discussion of the facts apart from the expression of any feelings you are experiencing. When tensions are high, avoid escalating the conflict by limiting yourself to the facts.

Later, think on the emotional impact of the disagreement, how you handled it, and your emotional triggers. Taking some time to reflect on your feelings without getting caught up in the moment may give you with valuable knowledge that will help you grow. To promote productive debate and avoid personal assaults, focus on facts first and sentiments second. Don't be afraid of uncomfortable conversations; overcoming them together will enhance your bond.

<u>There are no perfect relationships or friendships</u>
Respect others for who they are, and be loyal to yourself. Remember that not all difficult conversations end in resolution, so be patient to yourself if the conversation completely unravels. Remember to feel empathy for the other person and let them know you still care about them later. When you understand your boundaries and respect the

other person's emotions and points of view, you will have a much more fruitful conversation and may be able to save the relationship.

These challenging chats may feel like boiling in your own pudding at first, but the emotional ties will be far stronger in the long run. In fact, getting these conversations out of the way with love and respect for the other person can allow you to fully enjoy your holiday celebrations.

Conclusion

If you frequently find yourself unintentionally interrupting other people, there may be several factors at play. It could indicate that you're merely waiting for your chance to speak or that you're not really present at the moment. Whatever the cause, though, there's always room for improvement in terms of finding greater equilibrium and improving listening skills.

It's also something you can change rather rapidly. In fact, many people may start modifying their behavior the moment they decide to change. Motivation will improve once you understand the need to change ineffective behaviors such as interrupting and not listening. With some effort and mindfulness, you'll see the benefits of becoming a better listener very fast.

There are quite a few. Learning to be a better listener and managing your need to interrupt helps you avoid misinterpretation and makes the person you're listening to feel important. Listening well is the cornerstone of excellent communication, which is the most important aspect of any healthy relationship. It also makes conversations more enjoyable because they are less likely to be one-sided. So, with that in mind, here are a few tips for becoming a better listener.

Notice When You're Interrupting
To begin, the easiest method to break an interrupting habit is to become more conscious of it, particularly in situations when it is most likely to occur. Do you interrupt friends who call to share a story? Or do you step on the end of people's sentences at work?

The next time, you can say, 'I'm sorry, I just interrupted you. This communicates to the other person that you are aware of your behavior and aim to improve. From there, you can gradually become more mindful.

Simply being aware of your impulse to interject is the first step. It may feel unpleasant as you develop this awareness, but try to see how long you can remain in silence without quickly leaping in. As you practice this ability, you'll notice that your tolerance improves.

Do one thing at a time
While it is not always possible to accomplish one thing at a time, try not to multitask while listening to someone; you may find that you have an easier time absorbing what they are saying.

Act interested by making and maintaining eye contact with the person you're listening to. Listening and paying attention becomes much more difficult when you are distracted by other things going on around you. So remind yourself to be present while listening, as this will help you stay focused. When you're concentrated, you're less likely to interrupt others.

Wait to formulate your ideas
Interrupting might occur when you are overly preoccupied with planning your next words rather than listening to the current discourse. Instead of waiting your turn to speak, "pay close attention to what the speaker is saying. Let that sink in. Wait a beat before responding.

Look them in the eye
Interrupting is more common when you become lost in your thoughts and forget you're having a two-way conversation. You can establish a deeper connection with someone if you remember to look them in the eye. By looking the individual in the eye, you convey the following message: I am paying attention, caring, and listening.

You can do this at work, out with friends, or when conversing with your partner; there are numerous times during the day when listening is essential. And doing so can help strengthen your relationships.

Reflect on what they said
There's another method to allow oneself that all-important beat before answering: reflect back on the content and emotion of what the speaker is saying before reacting or contributing. You can describe what they say briefly and then offer your opinion.

This is something you can and should do even if you disagree with what is being stated because interrupting is more likely in that situation. In fact, when individuals feel appreciated, they are more willing to listen to your point of view or position. When others do not feel recognized, they are likely to ignore your subsequent comments or words as a response.

Don't make assumptions
Similarly, before entering a conversation, do not assume you know what the other person or individuals are going to say, even if you believe you do. By not having predefined expectations, you force yourself to listen in order to gain more knowledge.

This trick can be extremely effective for overcoming the habit of interrupting others. It can be challenging at first, especially if you're accustomed to jumping to conclusions. But it's something you can start working on today and prioritize in the future.

Do not jump to solutions
It is normal to be more concerned with resolving an issue than with simply sitting back and listening to what someone is saying. However, if you want to be a better listener, the last thing you want to do is glaze over and turn inward while brainstorming alternative answers.

If you do, you may not be totally attentive since you are strategizing while they are speaking. Sometimes all individuals want and need is someone to listen without necessarily providing a solution. If they ask for your counsel, that's another story, and you can give it.

Even if it feels uncomfortable at first, remember that it is always acceptable to sit and take a breath before replying.

Make it all about them
It's normal to want to talk about yourself or share your own opinions. Furthermore, there is undoubtedly a place and time for it. However, if you want to listen, you should simply wait.

Assume a friend is telling you about a difficulty they're having. Rather than thinking about a reaction, try to comprehend their emotional state. For example, if a buddy informs you that they have lost their job, consider their circumstances and how it may affect them, rather than how you would feel if you were in their shoes.

This can help you break the habit of interrupting others or offering your thoughts too soon. Instead, put yourself in their position and maintain your attention on them for now.

Hold off on the questions

You're far more likely to interrupt if you're asking questions instead of listening. Put your attention on the person in front of you rather than questioning them. Allow them to talk. Whether it's a friend who needs to vent or a coworker who wants to share their thoughts, remember to listen first; you can always ask questions later.

Try the 80/20 rule

Another useful communication technique is the 80/20 rule. It's 80% listening to the folks you're talking to and 20% speaking. Once you reach the 20% level, it's time to calm down and let others speak.

Keep this in mind in instances where you'll need to listen and gather information, or when someone else is speaking. You don't have to do it all the time because your thoughts are also valuable, but it can be useful when you're trying to change an interrupting habit or demonstrate to someone that you're paying attention.

Enjoy the positive side effects

To stay motivated and keep up the excellent effort, see your discussions as experiments to explore how they differ and how your relationships might improve if you interrupt less frequently. See if people react differently to you and begin to open up more when they interact with you.

When you practice listening instead of interrupting all the time, you'll probably discover that all of your interactions become a lot more engaging, and you connect with others on a much deeper level. And that is definitely worth the effort.